The Eyes Of Time

Grace Sumeria

A Collection of Poetry

SoBe Grace | Brighton UK

Copyright 2018 by **Grace Sumeria**

The right of Grace Sumeria to be identified as the author of this work has been asserted by her in accordance with the Copyright, Designs & Patents Act 1988.

SoBe Grace Publishing:
www.sobegrace.com

The Eyes Of Time/ Grace Sumeria. -- 1st ed.

ISBN 978-1-9993024-0-5

This collection of poetry is dedicated to
all those souls who speak their truth,
who wish to,
and who will in the future.

Contents

My Time To Write 1
Parks 2
Starting From Nothing 4
Time 5
Endings 6
Rain 8
The Hole In Me 9
40% 10
Moon Gazing 12
The Invisible Thread 13
All About You 14
Conversations With Old Friends 16
I've Waited For This 18
When She Smiles 19
Absence 20
Learning 21
Given Up 22
My Eyes Hurt 23
With You I Feel Safe 24
The Eyes Of Time 25
The Motherland 26
Paths 29
Romance 30
It's In Our Bones 32
Thoughts Of Him 33

A Piece Of Me 34
His Pain, My Pain 36
I Never Cry 37
Running 38
No Place For A Lady 39
Hope 40
Parallel Universe 42
A Part Of You, Apart From You 44
I Love You 45
I Don't Belong Here 46
Blood 47
Your Silence 48
Somewhere, Nowhere 50
#metoo 52
Tears 53
It Was Never Lost 54
Willing 56
I Isolate 58
The Greatest Love Of All 59
Mahatma 60

My Time To Write

Now is my time
        to write
                to heal
                      to be.

I've been for others
        for so long.

Not knowing that I was giving
        a piece of my soul.

...every time I did not write
inside it was felt
        outside it was ignored.

No longer.

Now is my time.
My time to write.

Parks

As I sit, beneath you.
    I am reminded of the parks of my life.
The wide, open space
    which gave me nature in the city.
Which gave me a place to sit,
    to dream,
        to meet the boys of my life.

Private spaces.
    With a key belonging to our flat.
Public, shared spaces:
    football being played,
    picnics eaten.

Famous London landmarks.
Small Frankfurt parks,
    to sit and yearn the loss of love.

Coastal parks,
    I come to almost daily.
To sit beneath you
    and have your leaves shade me,
    from the sun which feeds me.

This place of light
> saving me,
> from the shadows which have become me.

And, as I sit, I realise
> That this has always been the way.

Parks have always been my
> connection to nature.

And that is what has saved me.

Thank you to all the green spaces I have known.
And thank you for keeping these
> green spaces
> in big, city places.

Starting From Nothing

I am starting from nothing, I had no love.
Learning to live, from a place of heart.

A life-long lesson, of self-love and compassion.

Children who weren't loved, have a hard time loving as adults.

I live that now.

I can only guess that happy, content feeling.
My cells hold no remembrance.

I mother myself, as best I can.

I cannot recollect love, so I start from nothing.
And gently learn and build, this life-long lesson.

Time

I wish I had spent more time with you
when you were here,
when you were near.

The times you wanted to simply sit;
to cuddle;
to be.

I was always doing,
rather than being.
Chasing my dream,
building my business.

Working...

What is life about?
Relationships, love, temporary moments.

What do we make it about?
Achieving, striving, future results.

I wish I had spent more time with you.

That wish remains…

Endings

The waves beating on the stones,
the sound a rumble.
Reminiscent of the thunder
of last night.

Our emotions heightened
as the lunar eclipse progressed.
Our feelings towards one another
starting to end,
as the fullness of the moon
allowed us to let go.

The blood, the red;
Just as the blood in our veins
flowed strongly;
flowed freely.

We saw red.
We shouted; cried;
caught up in our worry
of change.

The ocean shows us change,
As the waves come and go.
The last few weeks had been calm,
And now.
The huge wild horses
of this new lunar cycle.

The synchronicity of our next step.

Rain

I awake eagerly,
Has it rained during the night?
I walk to the window,
No such luck,
I see the dust, people walking
Looking tired, mostly skin and bones;
Dirty,
I see an old man looking up into the sky,
Watching the deceiving clouds
When will it rain?

People in poverty with grey faces,
No way of getting clean.
Animals moving along the street
Looking for scraps of food to eat
The hot, hot sun beating down on their backs.
The woman fetching water from the well,
It is almost dry
How will she feed her husband and six children?
No water in the river, no water in the well
No water anywhere.
When will it rain?

The Hole In Me

There's a hole in my heart
      where love should be.

There's a hole in my heart
      where you should be.

I feel this hole in my heart
      every day.

The emptiness, the loss,
      the non-whole of me.

The hole...
                        in me.

40%

40% of women
    who experience infertility
        have suicidal thoughts.

How can I be sure
    That I will survive
        Given those stats?

How can I build myself up
    Strengthen myself
        To live

Everyday
    Every morning
        Every night

So that I become
    someone with joy
    and not merely a number.

So that I become
    a survivor
    a warrior

So that I become
>	someone with purpose
>	and not simply existing.

So that I become
>	me again
>	>	before all this.

The national fertility charity, Fertility Network UK, did a survey in 2016 to coincide with National Fertility Awareness Week and it revealed that over 40% of women experiencing infertility had suicidal thoughts.

Moon Gazing

She looked at the moon
Knowing it was the wise one.
The all-seeing.
All-knowing.
And she wept
For all that is and all that was...
And with this release
This deeply felt letting go
She felt her freedom.

The Invisible Thread

Little one.
        You were abandoned.

A babe making her own way.
Relying on herself;
Reprimanded for making wrong decisions;
Self-esteem lessening through the years.
Pulling herself up
To have herself brought down with
        one word or sentence.

From you, sweet mama.

The bond that wasn't there...
        is there.
The invisible thread.
Moving between us.

Sweet mama,
        Let your words heal...
                ...not hurt.

All About You

I loved him,
    you knew that.

He was everything to me,
    but not to you.

You pulled me away,
    from him.

Putting thoughts into my head...
    'He's not for you...'
    'You're better..'
    'He's not good enough...'

But the fact is,
    he was good enough.

He loved me,
    and that should have been enough.

It was enough for me,
    to be loved and cherished.
After always trying with you,
    and never receiving.

Maybe you never wanted me happy.

...because if a person could give me something,
   you couldn't.
...what would that say?

   About you.

Conversations With Old Friends

Conversations with old friends
are rich as we reflect on days gone by.

Conversations with old friends
are tender as we recall our feelings.

Conversations with old, dear friends.

You remember my writing,
              my poems,
                          my love.

I had forgotten
       the healing power of the word.

And it comes back to me.

The love I aways had of writing.

And I promise myself (and to you, dear friend)
       that I will start writing again.

I will start believing for that 17 year old.

I will start believing in this 44 year old.

And I will start writing
                and healing
                              and come back.

I've Waited For This

Sweet babe, the way you look at me
Sweet babe, the way you touch me
Sweet babe.

I've waited so long
    for this.

The feeling I get when you hold my hand
The feeling I get when you touch my face.
The feeling.
    I get.

I've waited a lifetime
and longer.
    for this.

Your look, your embrace, your touch, your kiss.
You.
Sweet babe.

I've waited so long
    for this.

And now I have it,
I'm scared.

When She Smiles

She looks downcast, she looks sad.
Her eyes tell so much, and so little.
She is beautiful when she smiles.

She loves looking, she loves sights.
Others cannot keep their eyes off her,
When she smiles.

She has energy, she has aura.
She has magic,
When she smiles.

Oh beautiful girl, why look so sad?
Keep smiling, keep beautiful.
You have the world,
And the world has you,
When you smile.

Absence

'Do you know him?' She asked,
         as she heard the news of George Michael passing.

Disbelief and then a wave of sadness.

My teenage walls had been full of Wham posters,
The radio blaring out my '80s sounds,
The Smash Hits at the ready for lyrics.

'Yes I knew him.' – what else was there to say?

Another example of her absence in my life.
Her disinterest in   ...me.

Her busyness of life and making a living.
Her self-centredness.
Her simply not wanting to engage with me.

The reasons don't matter.
All that matters is the realisation ...again
         that yes she was indeed absent.

And that layer of sadness returns.

Learning

What I learned from you,
        dear mama...

That I was never enough
        so my confidence is low.

That I cannot trust people
        so now I have no friends.

That other people are better
        so now my life is a competition.

That it's only worth doing if the rewards are high
        so now I'm in a job I hate.

That whatever I do
        you will never value me.

And validation from you
        will be my life-long mission.

The end.

Given Up

I've given up
On my life.

I feel tired,
Broken,
Done.

No energy,
No motivation.

I've given up.

A change is coming, they say...
New beginnings,
New energy,
New life.

But... sometimes...
When you've given up
it is just that.

My Eyes Hurt

My eyes hurt ...from the tears,
      from seeing,
      from the pain,
      from looking back.

To the future we go.

With You I Feel Safe

With you I feel safe,
With you I feel secure,
With you, in my heart, I am alive,
I am free to do as I wish,
I can be what I am and all that I will be.
My potential is fulfilled.
People can say what they please,
But with you by my side, I feel safe.
No more limitations or opportunities missed,
Everything is perfect now that you are here -
With me.
I feel safe, I feel secure.
I am alive.
No more goodbyes,
No more regrets.
Life is adorable,
With you I feel safe.

The Eyes Of Time

As life bubbles before me,
I grow tired.

The excitement of the young faces,
the weariness of my lines.

Do my eyes see the same?
Or have they taken on years of pain
and now see differently?

Those young, blue eyes see fresh.
These old, brown eyes...
      see...

They see further, behind the facade.
They see in terms of experience,
      of knowledge, of wisdom.

They see what those fresh eyes cannot;
they have seen what those young faces
      will never see.

A different time, a different era.
Time which will never come again.

The Motherland

The Motherland;
>a place of hope...
The Motherland;
>a place of love...
The Motherland;
>a place of mother...

But instead I find
>a mother who cannot love;
>a mother for whom I will never be enough;
>a mother in name only, not in heart.

I will never be welcome
>and accepted,
>>by the people who needed me here.

My children were promised riches
>and instead born into poverty.
In some ways their prospects are less
>than mine.

I was a child when I came over.
My parents, grandparents, elders
Always talking about the promises of the
Motherland.

'You could drop a fountain pen on the streets of London

and the police would hand it back to you. ¹

Such a golden country
overseen by the beautiful, young queen.

Such a golden country
we were happy to come here.

And came we did.
But live we did not.

Given rooms in houses nobody else wanted.
Paying for the privilege
To share one room
No water, no gas.

No blacks, no Irish, no dogs.

It was the way, it was what we found.
We became trapped in poverty
     and in discrimination.

Yes the prospects in our birth countries had been low.
But we were educated, we were hard-working.
We could have made something of ourselves
     if we hadn't been lied to.
We could have flourished
     if it wasn't for the brain-drain.

We had to make the best of here.
Most working in hard, manual jobs.
Looking after the old and sick no-one else wanted to.

Seeing the differences between reality and
what we had learned about the golden country,
    The Motherland.

Did we dream those school classes,
where we had learned about the fountain pen?

I receive no warmth, no love, no care
    from the people.
So when I can, I go back to sunshine.
To receive the warmth I need
to live in this motherland.

No longer a place of mother,
    but a place I simply exist.

Paths

The paths we take
Oh soul, the paths we take.
In this journey of life.

I came to this via that path.
The opportunity taken,
Another possibility in the wind.

That path would have been different
Taken me somewhere...
    ...else.

This path brings me here...
    ...to this.

Romance

No, not empty gestures such as giving flowers,
But gestures with meaning behind them,
Buying flowers on the way home to say 'I love you',
Flowers to match the sparkle in her eyes,
Or before a business trip to keep her company.

Walks in the park or on the beach,
Holding hands; 'at ease with one another',
And with nature.

Talking together about the meaningful,
and the meaningless.
Gazing into each other's eyes and not talking.

Rome

Spooning in bed, sweet kisses at the neck.
Lying in on a Sunday morning,
Reading the papers together or napping.

Praying together; staying together.

Trying to understand the differences,
But accepting the person for who they are,
and all that they will be.

Making an effort with friends and family.

Making time to see each other.
Trying new things together. Dancing.

Being happy when together,
But not feeling alone when apart.

Being your real, true person.
And finding your real, true partner
To have your happy ending with.

It's In Our Bones

It's in our bones
        the way they put us down.
It's in our bones
        the way they tied us up.
It's in our bones
        the beating
                the cries
                        the hurt
It's in our bones.

I see now
        the pain is deep.
I see now
        why I cannot cry.
I see now
        the strength.
I see...

It's in our bones.
Yes!

And.
I.
Break.
Free.

Thoughts Of Him

I loved him so completely,
I had put my heart and soul into the relationship,
Then one day....
              It's gone.
Never to return again,
Broken promises and shattered dreams;
No longer seeing a bright, rosy future,
Just taking each day as it comes
And as it goes, nothing to show for it
Only thoughts,
Thoughts of him.

A Piece Of Me

Every time I gave to others,
I gave a piece of myself.

Over time, my self depleted, vanished.
No wonder.

My self was not replenished,
Not given what it needed.

Love, compassion, care.
Yes!

And also...

My soul's need to express
     through words,
          through the medium of being a writer.

An unknown for me:
     new territory, strange lands.

But in a way   *home.*

Always knowing it was there,
but not knowing
or not giving
It   to my self,
        my soul.

Can I do it?
Can I write?

Can I be it?
Be this writer self?

Time will tell
As I give myself this container
of space.

Time will tell
as I give a piece of me,

Back to my self.

His Pain, My Pain

The metal mesh
      stung my skin,
As you pushed me
      against the fence.
I drew in breath
      'keep calm, keep calm'
The blows came...
      ...and went.

I Never Cry

The sounds of cries.
    And then,
        the fades.
As the child knows
    no-one is coming.

Brought into a world
    where its needs are not met.

Grows up and learns,
    not to trust.

Self-reliance is the way...
not to be confused
by independence,
    or freedom.

When you only have you;
There is no-one to hear
the cries,
    and the sound stops
    and never comes again.

Running

Running, running,
      running away.

That's what I do.

Did I learn this from you,
      dear mama?
Did I learn your narcissistic ways?

I need a home,
      need grounding.
But instead,
      I run away.

No Place For A Lady

It's no place for a lady, he said.
Crowded, smoky, too much beer
Bodies pressed together dancing
No room to move
Music too loud to talk.
So he's a gentleman,
But I'm no lady!

Hope

She watched
As the Wall
Came Down.

Artists' beautiful landscapes,
Hate graffiti
All mingled into one.

That concrete monstrosity
Which had kept us apart,
Now coming down.

Different lives
From one side to the other,
Now one.

Learning to live together,
Work together,
Learning to forget.

All those lost lives,
All those lost dreams
Not in vain.

We would be one city,
Have one voice;
Gone was the sorrow.

Around her was happiness
And hope
Of what would be.

Parallel Universe

I like to dream, sweet child.
I like to believe
      there's a parallel universe.
Somewhere, where we are together.

Where we are living
      and laughing
           and loving.

A place where the two of us
      can bathe in goodness.
Where there are no bad memories,
           no hurt,
                no loss.

Only laughter
      and love
           and life.

Where the two of us are bonded
      by the blood we share.

Where I see my features in you,
And the way you hold yourself
      is like looking in the mirror.

A parallel universe
> taking me away from the hurt
> of this existence.

A parallel universe
> I can believe in, sweet child.

A Part Of You, Apart From You

Oh mama,
    I need your love,
        Your comfort,
            I came from you,
                A part of you…
            Apart from you,
        That is the way it is,
    In this life.

I Love You

I love your eyes,
I love your smile,
I love your hair,
I love the way you wink at me,
And press your lips together as you give me a kiss.

You are so beautiful.
Both inside and out,
Both outside and in.

You are so beautiful,
And you are all mine,
Mine to love, mine to care for.
Mine forever
And ever and ever,
For you are me!

I Don't Belong Here

They came to our countries,
And took them over.
Into our homes, into our lives,
And ran them.
Now we're here, in this
Better country,
Living as them, learning as them,
But we're not one of them.
I want to go home to where I belong,
Where there are no barriers because of race.
Where everyone is the same -
One.

Blood

The blood flowing through me
                was my ancestors.

The people you tortured
                and raped
                        and hung.

That blood flows freely
                as I awaken.

Awaken to the truth of who I am.

And I see you.

And the blood flows.

Your Silence

I told you,
so you could tell.
I opened up to you,
to help myself.

I knew it was wrong, but too young
to know what to do,
I told you.

You could help.
You would know.
You would make the ills of the world better.

But rather...
you did not.

You did not tell.
You did not try to help me.

I was abused
And you were silence,
Your unwillingness to tell, to help me
gain justice,
from the abuser.

Your silence caused me harm,
additional pain;
in a way more abuse
                    to me.

I told you,
so you could tell.
Your silence spoke volumes.

My open self
was closed to the world,

Never to trust again.

Somewhere, Nowhere

1991

She looked so cold sitting there,
A pink woolly hat on her head
And a carrier bag by her side,
She looked like someone's grandmother
I hurried past, I had somewhere to go,
How many other people had gone past
Glancing at her once, not looking.

2018

27 years later
I still have her face in my memory.
Red skin, pink hat
Sitting alone
On a London street.
The guilt I felt as I hurried past.
My teenage self not fully comprehending
what I could do.

When I see cold faces now
I give a smile,
some change,
a cup of tea or coffee.
Or a silent blessing as I walk past.
I look, I see, not glance.
I don't hurry past. I am here.
There is nowhere to go.

#metoo

I came to you for lessons
        of the music kind.
What I learned was lessons
        of the male kind.

Using your power and influence
        over me.
You approached and put your hand down
        my blouse.

Shock, horror,
        numb, numb, numb

And the music played on.

Tears

For years I couldn't cry,
the tears wouldn't come.

Unlike my 20s,
when they flowed freely.

But now I cry again,
big tears.

The floodgates open,
I am broken.

Tears rush down,
they cleanse.

They come now,
to heal me.

It Was Never Lost

What will other people think?
    Does it matter?

It won't look good.
    Does it matter?

He's not for you...

So I proceeded through life
    not wanting to rock the boat,
    or stand out.

The boyfriends I had didn't last;
    two weeks here,
      a few months there.

Knowing that no one would ever be good enough,
    for you.
Even though they were perfect,
    for me.

I saw others get their dreams.
    Be with their loves.
        Grow happy.

I carried on searching...
...and what I didn't realise
was that I was searching
for your lost love...

for the love I've never felt from you.

This never came,
        and now I know.

It was never there,

        so never lost.

Willing

I wanted you so
        oh little one

Wanted to feel you,
        to love you,
        to cherish you.

I would be healed by you,
        I only notice that now.

Now that I know
        my own childhood wounds.

Now that I know
        that children teach.

That they heal our inner child.
        That they are sent so we can fully love.

Not having this outward lesson
        I must learn to inner listen.

To hear my inner child myself.
        To love myself fully.

It will be a life-long lesson.
    Just as, having children would have been.

When you are willing to learn
    I will be here, she says.

'Please be willing'
    I listen...

I Isolate

I isolate,
      I run,
           I have no roots,
                  I wander,
this is what you taught me,
        dear mama.

The Greatest Love Of All

The love within yourself is the greatest love of all.
It is a love which cannot be made.
A love which cannot die.
It is within all of us, and needs to be nurtured.
Encouraged to grow and prosper.
At the end, the love emitted;
Can be greater than oneself.
It can be the aura, the light;
The brightness around a holy person.
It is a never-ending quality,
A part within yourself to constantly cherish,
Never let the feeling of loving go.
The love within yourself will be your best friend.
It is the greatest love of all.

Mahatma

Today I break free.
Today I become me.

Soul, I've been healing;
    ...deep, deep healing.

From times past, from childhood,
    from NOW-hood.

Laying in bed this morning, I realised
    my soul is great.
It is the Maha Atma...

Soul, at school they used to call me
    Mahatma;
using it as an insult,
    drawing on my skin colour.

I burned, not knowing the meaning,
    only the offence I felt.
It would shut me away,
Close me to my   *greatness*.

But, *Soul*
>> today I break free,
>> today I become me.

Yes I can be the Mahatma,
In the wonderful meaning of the word.
I can reach into my greatness,
Reach into my soul,
And bring it out to play, to flourish,
>> to heal.

Today I become me.

About the Author

Grace Sumeria started writing in a diary in her teenage years. At age 16, she discovered poetry whilst studying English Literature.

Her love of writing poetry continued through the years and in addition to her journal reflections, writing poems allowed her to observe life.
Now in her 40s, Grace uses writing as a healing tool and has fully embraced her writing life.

Writing under this nom de plume has allowed Grace to address themes of her life, which otherwise would have remained hidden: her relationship with her narcissistic mother, healing the deep sadness she feels,
childlessness not by choice, social injustice, abuse, love, freedom.

Writing poetry has allowed her to reach into her inner depths and bring about the healing she needed.

Grace lives on the South Coast of England with her husband. *The Eyes Of Time* is her first poetry collection.

www.ingramcontent.com/pod-product-compliance
Lightning Source LLC
Chambersburg PA
CBHW060541080526
44586CB00012B/811